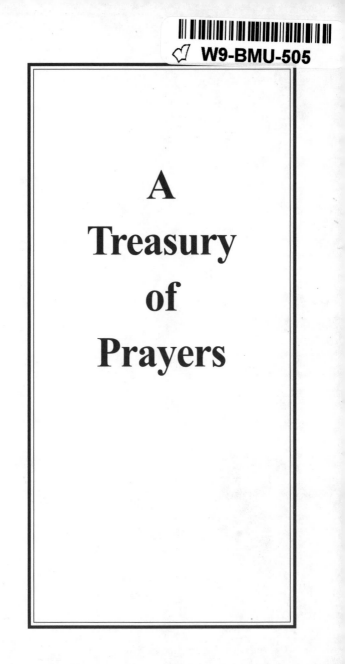

A
Treasury
of
Prayers

A
Treasury
of
Prayers

James W. Albrecht, *Editor*

Scepter Publishers

Nihil Obstat:

      Daniel V. Flynn, J.C.D.
      Censor librorum

Imprimatur:

      ✠James P. Mahoney, D.D.
      Vicar General
      Archdiocese of New York

March 3, 1975

SCEPTER PUBLISHERS
P.O. Box 1270
Princeton, NJ 08542

ISBN 1-889334-34-0

Contents

Introduction

"A good Christian acquires his mettle, with the help of grace, in the training-ground of prayer. But prayer, our life-giving nourishment, is not limited to one form alone. Our heart will find an habitual expression in words, in the vocal prayers taught us by God himself — the Our Father — or by his angels —the Hail Mary. On other occasions, we will use the time-proven words that have expressed the piety of millions of our brothers in the faith: prayers from the liturgy — *lex orandi;* or others whose source is the love of an ardent heart, like the antiphons to our Lady: *Sub tuum praesidium; Memorare; Salve, Regina....*

"There will be other occasions on which all we'll need will be two or three words, said with the quickness of a dart, *iaculata*: ejaculatory prayers, aspirations that we learn from a careful reading of Christ's life: 'Lord if you will, you can make me clean' (Mt 8:2). 'Lord, you know all things, you know that I love you' (Jn 21:17). 'Lord, I do believe, but help my unbelief' (Mk

9:23), strengthen my faith. 'Lord, I am not worthy' (Mk 8:8). 'My Lord and my God' (Jn 20:28)…or other short phrases, full of affection, that spring from the soul's intimate fervor and correspond to the different circumstances of each day." — Blessed Josemaría Escrivá, *Christ Is Passing By*, no. 119.

Sign of the Cross

In nomine Patris, et Filii, et Spiritus Sancti. Amen.

Per signum crucis de inimicis nostris libera nos, Deus noster. In nomine Patris, et Filii, et Spiritus Sancti. Amen.

Lord's Prayer

Pater noster, qui es in caelis, sanctificetur nomen tuum. Adveniat regnum tuum. Fiat voluntas tua, sicut in coelo et in terra. Panem nostrum quotidianum da nobis hodie. Et dimitte nobis debita nostra, sicut et nos dimittimus debitoribus nostris. Et ne nos inducas in tentationem: sed libera nos a malo. Amen.

Hail Mary

Ave, Maria, gratia plena, Dominus tecum; benedicta tu in mulieribus, et benedictus fructus ventris tui, Jesus.

Sancta Maria, Mater Dei, ora pro nobis peccatoribus, nunc et in hora mortis nostrae. Amen.

Sign of the Cross

In the name of the Father, and of the Son, and of the Holy Spirit. Amen.

By the sign of the cross deliver us from our enemies, you who are our God. In the name of the Father, and of the Son, and of the Holy Spirit. Amen.

Lord's Prayer

Our Father, who art in heaven, hallowed be thy name; thy kingdom come; thy will be done on earth as it is in heaven. Give us this day our daily bread; and forgive us our trespasses as we forgive those who trespass against us, and lead us not into temptation, but deliver us from evil. Amen.

Hail Mary

Hail, Mary, full of grace, the Lord is with thee, blessed art thou among women, and blessed is the fruit of thy womb, Jesus. Holy Mary, Mother of God, pray for us sinners, now and at the hour of our death. Amen.

Glory Be

Gloria Patri, et Filio, et Spiritui Sancto. Sicut erat in principio et nunc et semper et in saecula saeculorum. Amen.

Blessing before Meals

Benedic, Domine, nos et haec tua dona quae de tua largitate sumus sumpturi. Per Christum Dominum nostrum. Amen.

(*Add for midday*): Mensae coelestis participes faciat nos, Rex aeternae gloriae. Amen.

(*Add for evening*): Ad coenam vitae aeternae perducat nos, Rex aeternae gloriae. Amen.

Grace after Meals

Agimus tibi gratias, omnipotens Deus, pro universis beneficiis tuis, qui vivis et regnas in saecula saeculorum. Amen.

Deus det nobis suam pacem. *Et vitam aeternam.* Amen.

Glory Be

Glory be to the Father, and to the Son, and to the Holy Spirit. As it was in the beginning, is now, and ever shall be, world without end. Amen.

Blessing before Meals

Bless us, O Lord, and these your gifts which we are about to receive from your bounty, through Christ our Lord. Amen.

Grace after Meals

We give you thanks, almighty God, for all your benefits, who live and reign, world without end. Amen.

The Confiteor

Confiteor Deo omnipotenti, beatae Mariae, semper Virgini, beato Michaeli archangelo, beato Joanni Baptistae, sanctis apostolis Petro et Paulo et omnibus sanctis: quia peccavi nimis cogitatione, verbo et opere: mea culpa, mea culpa, mea maxima culpa. Ideo precor beatam Mariam semper Virginem, beatum Michaelem archangelum, beatum Joannem Baptistam, sanctos apostolos Petrum et Paulum, et omnes sanctos, orare pro me ad Dominum Deum nostrum.

Confiteor Deo omnipotenti et vobis fratres, quia peccavi nimis cognitatione, verbo, opere et omissione: mea culpa, mea culpa, mea mixima culpa. Ideo precor beatam Mariam semper Viginem, omnes angelos et sanctos, et vos, fratres, orare pro me ad Dominum Deum nostrum.

To the Holy Spirit

Veni, Sancte Spiritus, reple tuorum corda fidelium, et tui amoris in eis ignem incende. Emitte Spiritum tuum, et creabuntur. *Et renovabis faciem terrae.*

Oremus. Deus, qui corda fidelium Sancti Spiritus illustratione docuisti, da nobis in eodem Spiritu recta sapere, et de ejus semper consolatione gaudere. Per Christum Dominum nostrum. *Amen.*

The Confiteor

I confess to almighty God, to blessed Mary ever Virgin, to blessed Michael the archangel, to blessed John the Baptist, to the holy apostles Peter and Paul, and to all the saints, that I have sinned exceedingly in thought, word and deed, through my fault, through my fault, through my most grievous fault. Therefore, I beseech blessed Mary ever Virgin, blessed Michael the archangel, blessed John the Baptist, the holy apostles Peter and Paul, and all the saints, to pray to the Lord our God for me.

I confess to almighty God, and to you, my brothers and sisters, that I have sinned through my own fault in my thoughts and in my words, in what I have done, and in what I have failed to do; and I ask blessed Mary, ever Virgin, all the angels and saints, and you, my brothers and sisters, to pray for me to the Lord our God.

To the Holy Spirit

Come, O Holy Spirit, fill the hearts of your faithful and enkindle in them the fire of your love. Send forth your Spirit, and they shall be created. And you shall renew the face of the earth.

Let us pray. O God, who has taught the hearts of the faithful by the light of the Holy Spirit, grant that by the gift of the same Spirit we may be always truly wise and ever rejoice in his consolation. Through Christ our Lord. Amen.

Adoro Te Devote

Adóro te devóte, látens Déitas,
Quae sub his figúris vere látitas.
Tibi se cor meum totum súbjicit,
Quia te contémplans totum déficit.

Visus, tactus, gustus in te fállitur,
Sed audítu solo tuto créditur.
Credo quiquid dixit Dei Fílius;
Nil hoc verbo Veritátis vérius.

In Cruce latébat sola Déitas.
At hic latet simul et humánitas.
Ambo tamen crédens atque cónfitens;
Peto quod petívit latro paénitens.

Plagas, sicut Thomas, non intúeor;
Deum tamen meum te confíteor.
Fac me tibi semper magis crédere,
In te spem habére, te dilígere.

O memoriále mortis Dómini!
Panis vivus, vitam praéstans hómini!
Praésta meae menti de te vívere
Et te illi semper dulce sápere.

Pie pellicáne, Jesu Dómine,
Me immúndum munda tuo sánguine,
Cujus una stilla salvum fácere
Totum mundum quit ab omni scélere.

Jesu, quem velátum nunc aspício,
Oro fiat illud quod tam sítio:
Ut te reveláta cérnens fácie,
Visu sim beátus tuae glóriae. Amen.

Adoro Te Devote

O Godhead hid, devoutly I adore thee,
Who truly art within the forms before me;
To thee my heart I bow with bended knee,
As failing quite in contemplating thee.

Sight, touch and taste in thee are each deceived;
The ear alone most safely is believed.
I believe all the Son of God has spoken:
Than Truth's own word there is no truer token.

God only on the cross lay hid from view,
But here lies hid at once the manhood too:
And I, in both professing my belief,
Make the same prayer as the repentant thief.

Thy wounds, as Thomas saw, I do not see;
Yet thee confess my Lord and God to be.
Make me believe thee ever more and more,
In thee my hope, in thee my love to store.

O thou, memorial of our Lord's own dying!
O living bread, to mortals life supplying!
Make thou my soul henceforth on thee to live;
Ever a taste of heavenly sweetness give.

O loving Pelican! O Jesus Lord!
Unclean I am, but cleanse me in thy blood:
Of which a single drop, for sinners spilt,
Can purge the entire world from all its guilt.

Jesus, whom for the present veiled I see,
What I so thirst for, do vouchsafe to me:
That I may see thy countenance unfolding,
And may be blest thy glory in beholding. Amen.

Hail, Holy Queen

Salve, Regina; mater misericordiae: vita, dulcedo et spes nostra, salve. Ad te clamamus exsules, filii Evae. Ad te suspiramus, gementes et flentes in hac lacrymarum valle. Eia ergo, advocata nostra illos tuos misericordes oculos ad nos converte. Et Jesum, benedictum fructum ventris tui, nobis post hoc exsilium ostende. O clemens: O pia: O dulcis Virgo Maria. Ora pro nobis, sancta Dei Genitrix. *Ut digni efficiamur promissionibus Christi.*

The Angelus

Angelus Domini, nuntiavit Mariae.
Et concepit de Spiritu Sancto. Ave Maria.

Ecce ancilla Domini.
Fiat mihi secundum verbum tuum. Ave Maria.

Et Verbum caro factum est.
Et habitavit in nobis. Ave Maria.

Ora pro nobis, sancta Dei Genitrix.
Ut digni efficiamur promissionibus Christi.

Oremus. Gratiam tuam, quaesumus. Domine, mentibus nostris infunde; ut qui, angelo nuntiante, Christi Filii tui incarnationem cognovimus, per passionem ejus et crucem, ad resurrectionis gloriam perducamur. Per eumdem Christum Dominum nostrum. Amen.

Hail, Holy Queen

Hail, Holy Queen, mother of mercy, hail, our life, our sweetness, and our hope! To you do we cry, poor banished children of Eve! To you do we send up our sighs, mourning and weeping in this vale of tears! Turn then, most gracious advocate your eyes of mercy toward us; and after this, our exile, show unto us the blessed fruit of your womb, Jesus! O clement, O loving, O sweet Virgin Mary! Pray for us, O holy Mother of God. *That we may be made worthy of the promises of Christ.*

The Angelus

The angel of the Lord declared unto Mary;
And she conceived of the Holy Spirit. Hail Mary.

Behold the handmaid of the Lord.
Be it done unto me according to your word. Hail Mary.

And the Word was made flesh:
And dwelt among us. Hail Mary.

Pray for us, O holy Mother of God
That we may be made worthy of the promises of Christ.

Let us pray. Pour forth, we beseech you, O Lord, your grace into our hearts, that we, to whom the incarnation of Christ, your Son, was made known by the message of an angel, may by his passion and cross, be brought to the glory of his resurrection, through the same Christ our Lord. Amen.

The Regina Coeli

Regina coeli, laetare. Alleluia.
Quia quem meruisti portare. Alleluia.

Resurrexit, sicut dixit. Alleluia.
Ora pro nobis, Deum. Alleluia.

Gaude et laetare, Virgo Maria. Alleluia.
Quia surrexit Dominus vere. Alleluia.

Oremus. Deus, qui per resurrectionem Filii tui Domini nostri Jesu Christi, mundum laetificare dignatus es: praesta, quaesumus; ut, per ejus Genitricem Virginem Mariam, perpetuae capiamus gaudia vitae. Per eumdem Christum Dominum nostrum. Amen.

Psalm 2

Ant. Regnum eius regnum sempiternum est, et omnes reges servient ei et obedient (*T.P. Alleluia*).

Quare fremuerunt gentes, et populi meditati sunt inania?

Astiterunt reges terrae, et principes convenerunt in unum adversus Dominum et adversus Christum ejus.

"Dirumpamus vincula eorum et proiciamus a nobis jugum ipsorum!"

Qui habitat in caelis, irridebit eos, Dominus subsannabit eos.

Tunc loquetur ad eos in ira sua et in furore suo conturbabit eos:

The Regina Coeli

Queen of heaven, rejoice! Alleluia.
For he whom you did merit to bear. Alleluia.

Has risen, as he said. Alleluia.
Pray for us to God. Alleluia.

Rejoice and be glad O Virgin Mary. Alleluia.
For the Lord is truly risen. Alleluia.

   Let us pray. O God who gave joy to the world through the resurrection of your Son our Lord Jesus Christ, grant, we beseech you, that through the intercession of the Virgin Mary, his Mother, we may obtain the joys of everlasting life, through the same Christ our Lord. Amen.

Psalm 2

Ant. His kingdom is a kingdom of all ages, and all kings shall serve and obey Him. (*P.T. Alleluia*).

Why have the Gentiles raged, and the people devised vain things? The kings of the earth stood up, and the princes met together, against the Lord, and against his Christ: "Let us break their bonds asunder; and let us cast away their yoke from us." He that dwells in heaven shall laugh at them; and the Lord shall deride them. Then shall he speak to them in his anger, and trouble them with his rage.

"Ego autem constitui regem meum super Sion, montem sanctum meum!"

Praedicabo decretum eius. Dominus dixit ad me: "Filius meus es tu; ego hodie genui te.

Postula a me, et dabo tibi gentes hereditatem tuam et possessionem tuam terminos terrae.

Reges eos in virga ferrea et tamquam vas figuili confringes eos."

Et nunc, reges, intellegite, erudimini qui judicatis terram.

Servite Domino in timore et exsultate ei cum tremore.

Apprehendite disciplinam, ne quando irascatur, et pereatis de via, cum exarserit in brevi ira eius. Beati omnes, qui confidunt in eo.

Gloria Patri....

Ant. Regnum eius regnum sempiternum est, et omnes reges servient ei et obedient (*T.P. Alleluia*).

V. Domine, exaudi orationem meam.

R. *Et clamor meus ad te veniat.*

(Priests add)

V. Dominus vobiscum.

R. *Et cum spiritu tuo.*

Oremus. Omnipotens sempiterne Deus, qui in dilecto Filio tuo, universorum Rege, omnia instaurare voluisti: concede propitius; ut cunctae familiae Gentium, peccati vulnere disgregatae, eius suavissimo subdantur imperio: Qui tecum vivit et regnat in unitate Spiritus Sancti Deus: per omnia saecula saeculorum. *Amen.*

But I am appointed king by him over Sion, his holy mountain, preaching his commandment. The Lord has said to me: "You are my son, this day have I begotten you. Ask of me, and I will give you the Gentiles for your inheritance, and the utmost parts of the earth for your possession. You shall rule them with a rod of iron and shall break them in pieces like a potter's vessel."

And now, O kings, understand: receive instruction, you that judge the earth. Serve the Lord with fear, and rejoice unto him with trembling. Embrace discipline, lest at any time the Lord be angry, and you perish from the just way. When his wrath shall be kindled in a short time, blessed are all they that trust in him. *Glory be....*

Ant. His kingdom is a kingdom of all ages and all kings shall serve and obey Him.

V. Lord, hear my prayer.

R. *And let my cry come to you.*

(Priests add)

V. The Lord be with you.

R. *And also with you.*

Let us pray. Almighty and everlasting God, who willed to restore all things in your beloved Son, the King of the whole world; grant in your mercy, that all the families of nations, torn apart by the wound of sin, may become subject to his most gentle rule, who, being God, lives and reigns with you in the unity of the Holy Spirit, world without end. *Amen.*

Psalm 51

Miserere mei, Deus, secundum magnam miseri-
cordiam tuam. Et secundum multitudinem
miserationum tuarum, dele iniquitatem meam.
Amplius lava me ab iniquitate mea: et a peccato
meo munda me. Quoniam iniquitatem meam ego
cognosco: et peccatum meum contra me est semper. Tibi soli peccavi, et malum coram te feci: ut
justificeris in sermonibus tuis, et vincas cum
judicaris.

Ecce enim in iniquitatibus conceptus sum: et
in peccatis concepit me mater mea. Ecce enim
veritatem dilexisti: incerta et occulta sapientiae
tuae manifestasti mihi. Asperges me hyssopo, et
mundabor: lavabis me, et super nivem dealbabor.

Auditui meo dabis gaudium et laetitiam: et
exsultabunt ossa humiliata. Averte faciem tuam
a peccatis meis: et omnes iniquitates meas dele.
Cor mundum crea in mea, Deus: et spiritum rec-
tum innova in visceribus meis. Ne projicias me
a facie tua: et spiritum sanctum tuum ne auferas
a me. Redde mihi laetitiam salutaris tui: et spiritu
principali confirma me. Docebo iniquos vias
tuas: et impii ad te convertentur.

Libera me de sanguinibus, Deus, Deus salutis
meae: et exsultabit lingua mea justitiam tuam.
Domine, labia mea aperies: et os meum an-
nuntiabit laudem tuam. Quoniam si voluisses
sacrificium, dedissem utique: holocaustis non

Psalm 51

Have mercy on me, O God, in your goodness; in the greatness of your compassion wipe out my offense. Thoroughly wash me from my guilt. For I acknowledge my offense, and my sin is before me always: "Against you only have I sinned, and done what is evil in your sight" — that you may be justified in your sentence, vindicated when you condemn. Indeed, in guilt was I born, and in sin my mother conceived me; behold, you are pleased with sincerity of heart, and in my inmost being you teach me wisdom.

Cleanse me of sin with hyssop, that I may be purified; wash me, and I shall be whiter than snow. Let me hear the sounds of joy and gladness; the bones you have crushed shall rejoice. Turn away your face from my sins, and blot out all my guilt.

A clean heart create for me, O God, and a steadfast spirit renew within me. Cast me not from your presence, and your holy spirit take not from me. Give me back the joy of your salvation, and a willing spirit sustain in me.

I will teach transgressors your ways, and sinners shall return to you. Free me from blood guilt, O God, my saving God; then my tongue shall revel in your justice. O Lord, open my lips, and my mouth shall proclaim your praise. For you are not pleased with sacrifices, should I offer a

delectaberis. Sacrificium Deo spiritu contribu-
latus: cor contritum, et humiliatum, Deus, non
despicies. Benigne fac, Domine, in bona vol-
untate tua Sion: ut aedificentur muri Jerusalem.

Tunc acceptabis sacrificium justitiae, obla-
tiones, et holocausta: tunc imponent super altare
tuum vitulos.

Some Aspirations

Domine, tu omnia nosti; tu scis quia amo te
(Jn 21:17).

Jesu, fili David, miserere mei (Mk 10:47).

Ecce ego, quia vocasti me (I Sam 3:6).

Credo, sed adiuva incredulitatem meam (Mk 9:24).

Adauge nobis fidem (Lk 17:5).

Illum oportet crescere, me autem minui (Jn 3:30).

Non voluntas mea, sed tua fiat (Mt 26:39).

Sine me nihil potestis facere (Jn 15:5)

Omnia possum in eo qui me confortat (Phil 4:13).

Dominus meus et Deus meus (Jn 20:28).

Quia tu es, Deus, fortitudo mea (Ps 42:2).

Sancta Maria, spes nostra, sedes sapientiae, ora pro
nobis

Sancta Maria, spes nostra, ancilla Domini, ora pro
nobis

Mater pulchrae dilectionis, filios tuos adiuva.

holocaust, you would not accept it. My sacrifice, O God, is a contrite spirit; a heart contrite and humbled, O God, you will not spurn.

Be bountiful, O Lord, to Sion in your kindness by rebuilding the walls of Jerusalem; then shall you be pleased with due sacrifices on your altar.

Some Aspirations

Lord, you know all things, you know that I love you.

Jesus, Son of David, have mercy on me!

Here I am, for you did call me.

I do believe; help my unbelief.

Increase our faith.

He must increase, but I must decrease.

Not as I will, but as you will.

Without me you can do nothing.

I can do all things in him who strengthens me.

My Lord and my God.

For you, O God, are my strength.

Holy Mary, our hope, seat of wisdom,
pray for us.

Holy Mary, our hope, handmaid of the Lord, pray for us.

Mother of fair love, help your children.

Cor Mariae dulcissimum, iter para tutum.

Jesu, Jesu, esto mihi semper Jesus.

Sancta Maria, stella orientis, filios tuos adiuva.

Sancta Maria, stella maris, filios tuos adiuva.

Cor Jesu sacratissimum, dona nobis pacem.

Deo omnis gloria.

Cor contritum, et humiliatum, Deus non despicies
(Ps 51:17).

Adauge nobis fidem, spem et caritatem.

Filius hominis non venit ut ministraretur ei, sed ut
ministraret (Mk 10:45).

Apud Deum omnia possibilia sunt (Mt 19:26).

Meus cibus est ut faciam voluntatem ejus qui misit
me, ut perficiam opus ejus (Jn 4:34).

Diligentibus Deum omnia cooperantur in bonum
(Rom 8:28).

Omnia in bonum.

Pauper servus et humilis.

Ago tibi gratias pro universis beneficiis tuis, etiam
ignotis.

Mandatum novum do vobis: ut diligatis invicem,
sicut dilexi vos, ut et vos diligatis invicem.

Cor mundum crea in me, Deus (Ps 51:10).

In te Domine, speravi: non confundar in aeternum
(Ps 31:1).

Sweet heart of Mary, prepare a safe way for us.

Jesus, Jesus, always be Jesus to me.

Holy Mary, star of the East, help your children.

Holy Mary, star of the sea, help your children.

Sacred heart of Jesus, grant us peace.

All the glory for God.

A heart contrite and humbled, O God, you will not spurn.

Increase our faith, hope and charity.

The Son of man has not come to be served but to serve.

With God all things are possible.

My food is to do the will of him who sent me, to accomplish his work.

For those who love God all things work together unto good.

All unto good.

A poor and lowly servant am I.

I give you thanks for all your benefits, even the unknown ones.

A new commandment I give you, that you love one another: that as I have loved you, you also love one another.

A clean heart create for me, O God.

In you, O Lord, I take refuge; let me never be put to shame.

Abba, Pater! (Gal 4:6).

Domine, ut videam (Lk 18:41).

Regina apostolorum, ora pro nobis.

Monstra te esse matrem.

Tantum dic verbo (Mt 8:8).

Domine, quid me vis facere? (Acts 9:6).

Doce nos amare.

To St. Michael

Sancte Michael archangele, defende nos in proelio, contra nequitiam et insidias diaboli esto praesidium. Imperet illi Deus, supplices de-precamur: tuque, Princeps militiae coelestis, Satanam aliosque spiritus malignos, qui ad perditionem animarum pervagantur in mundo, divina virtute, in infernum detrude. Amen.

Athanasian Creed

Quicumque vult salvus esse, ante omnia opus est, ut teneat catholicam fidem:

Quam nisi quisque integram inviolatamque servaverit, absque dubio in aeternum peribit.

Fides autem catholica haec est: ut unum Deum in Trinitate, et Trinitatem in unitate veneremur.

Neque confundentes personas, neque substan-tiam separantes.

Father, my Father.

Lord, that I may see.

Queen of apostles, pray for us.

Show you are our mother.

Say but the word.

Lord, what do you want me to do?

Teach us to love.

To St. Michael

St. Michael the archangel, defend us in battle; be our defense against the wickedness and snares of the devil. May God rebuke him, we humbly pray. And do you, O prince of the heavenly host, by the power of God thrust into hell Satan and all the evil spirits who prowl about the world for the ruin of souls. Amen.

Athanasian Creed

Whoever wishes to be saved must, above all, keep the Catholic faith, for unless a person keeps this faith whole and entire he will undoubtedly be lost forever.

This is what the Catholic faith teaches. We worship one God in the Trinity and the Trinity in unity; we distinguish among the persons, but we do not divide the substance. For the Father is a distinct person; the Son is a distinct person;

Alia est enim persona Patris, alia Filii, alia Spiritus Sancti:

Sed Patris, et Filii, et Spiritus Sancti una est divinitas, aequalis gloria, coaeterna majestas.

Increatus Pater, increatus Filius, increatus Spiritus Sanctus.

Immensus Pater, immensus Filius, immensus Spiritus Sanctus.

Aeternus Pater, aeternus Filius, aeternus Spiritus Sanctus.

Et tamen non tres aeterni, sed unus aeternus.

Sicut non tres increati, nec tres immensi, sed unus increatus, et unus immensus.

Similiter omnipotens Pater, omnipotens Filius, omnipotens Spiritus Sanctus.

Et tamen non tres omnipotentes, sed unus omnipotens.

Ita Deus Pater, Deus Filus, Desu Spiritus Sanctus.

Et tamen non tres dii, sed unus est Deus.

Ita Dominus Pater, Dominus Filius, Dominus Spiritus Sanctus.

Et tamen non tres Domini, sed unus est Dominus.

Quia, sicut singillatim unamquamque personam Deum ac Dominum confiteri christiana veritate compellimur: ita tres Deos aut Dominos dicere catholica religione prohibemur.

Pater a nullo est factus: nec creatus, nec genitus.

Filius a Patre solo est: non factus, nec creatus, sed genitus.

and the Holy Spirit is a distinct person. Still the Father and the Son and the Holy Spirit have one divinity, equal glory, and coeternal majesty. That the Father is, the Son is, and the Holy Spirit is. The Father is uncreated, the Son is uncreated, and the Holy Spirit is uncreated. The Father is boundless, the Son is boundless, and the Holy Spirit is boundless. The Father is eternal, the Son is eternal, and the Holy Spirit is eternal. Nevertheless, there are not three eternal beings, but one eternal being. Thus there are not three uncreated beings, nor three boundless beings, but one uncreated being and one boundless being.

Likewise, the Father is omnipotent, the Son is omnipotent, and the Holy Spirit is omnipotent. Yet there are not three omnipotent beings, but one omnipotent being. Thus the Father is God, the Son is God, and the Holy Spirit is God. But there are not three gods, but one God. The Father is lord, the Son is lord, and the Holy Spirit is lord. There are not three lords, but one Lord. For according to Christian truth, we must profess that each of the persons individually is God; and according to the Christian religion we are forbidden to say that there are three gods or three lords. The Father is not made by anyone, nor created by anyone, nor generated by anyone. The Son is not made nor created, but he is generated by the Father alone. The Holy Spirit is not made nor created nor generated, but proceeds from the Father and the Son.

Spiritus Sanctus a Patre et Filio non factus, nec creatus, nec genitus, sed procedens.

Unus ergo Pater, non tres Patres: unus Filius, non tres Filii: unus Spiritus Sanctus, non tres Spiritus Sancti.

Et in hac Trinitate nihil prius aut posterius, nihil maius aut minus: sed totae tres personae coaeternae sibi sunt et coaequales.

Ita ut per omnia, sicut jam supra dictum est, et unitas in Trinitate, et Trinitas in unitate veneranda sit.

Qui vult ergo salvus esse, ita de Trinitate sentiat.

Sed necessarium est ad aeternam salutem, ut incarnationem quoque Domini nostri Jesu Christi fideliter credat.

Est ergo fides recta ut credamus et confiteamur, quia Dominus noster Jesus Christus, Dei Filius, Deus et homo est.

Deus est ex substantia Patris ante saecula genitus: et homo est ex substantia matris in saeculo natus.

Perfectus Deus, perfectus homo: ex anima rationali et humana carne subsistens.

Aequalis Patri secundum divinitatem: minor Patre secundum humanitatem.

Qui, licet Deus sit et homo, non duo tamen, sed unus est Christus.

Unus autem non conversione divinitatis in carnem, sed assumptione humanitatis in Deum.

There is, then, one Father, not three fathers; one Son, not three sons, one Holy Spirit, not three holy spirits. In this Trinity, there is nothing greater, nothing less than anything else. But the entire three persons are coeternal and coequal with one another, so that, as we have said, we worship complete unity in the Trinity and the Trinity in unity. This, then, is what he who wishes to be saved must believe about the Trinity.

It is also necessary for eternal salvation that he believe steadfastly in the incarnation of our Lord Jesus Christ. The true faith is: we believe and profess that our Lord Jesus Christ, the son of God, is both God and man. As God he was begotten of the substance of the Father before time; as man he was born in time of the substance of his Mother. He is perfect God; and he is perfect man, with a rational soul and human flesh. He is equal to the Father in his divinity, but he is inferior to the Father in his humanity. Although he is God and man, he is not two but one Christ. And he is one, not because his divinity was changed into flesh, but because his humanity was assumed to God. He is one, not at all because of a mingling of substances, but because he is one person. As a rational soul and flesh are one man, so God and man are one Christ. He died for our salvation, descended into hell, arose from the dead on the third day, ascended into heaven, sits at the right hand of God

Unus omnino, non confusione substantiae, sed unitate personae.

Nam sicut anima rationalis et caro unus est homo: ita Deus et homo unus est Christus.

Qui passus est pro salute nostra: descendit ad inferos: tertia die resurrexit a mortuis.

Ascendit ad coelos, sedet ad dexteram Dei Patris omnipotentis: inde venturus est judicare vivos et mortuos.

Ad cujus adventum omnes homines resurgere habent cum corporibus suis: et reddituri sunt de factis propriis rationem.

Et qui bona egerunt, ibunt in vitam aeternam: qui vero mala, in ignem aeternum.

Haec est fides catholica, quam nisi quisque fideliter firmiterque crediderit, salvus esse non poterit.

the Father almighty, and from there he shall come to judge the living and the dead. At his coming, all men are to arise with their own bodies; and they are to give an account of their lives. Those who have done good deeds will go into eternal life; those who have done evil will go into everlasting fire.

This is the Catholic faith. Everyone must believe it, firmly and steadfastly; otherwise he cannot be saved.

Praying before the Blessed Sacrament

You are here in the chapel, but not alone, for Christ upon the altar is here with you—

There will indeed come another day, perhaps sooner than you think, when you will again be alone with Christ — the day when you shall leave father, mother, wife and children, friends, your hard-earned wealth, the pleasures of this world — the day when you feel your strength departing, and your senses closing out the world all about you, closing out all you may have cherished here in this life.

Then you will be ALONE with Christ, alone with Him for the last time upon earth, with Christ your saviour coming to reward you for your life of service, or with Christ your Judge, coming to ask an accounting of your stewardship.

Then, at long last, the great business of your soul's salvation will force itself upon you and you will realize then, if never before, that truly it profits a man nothing to gain the whole world and yet to suffer the loss of his own soul.

Do not wait, if you are wise, do not wait until that visit of Christ, to be alone with Him.

You are alone with Him now, in this chapel, in this church — and so speak to Him while you may.

Pray to Him now while you may, begging pardon from Him while yet you may, for later it may be too late.

Now He calls you from out of this tabernacle.

Have you something to say to Him?

Listen ... and Speak to Him ...

To please Me, it is not necessary to know much; all that is required is to love Me much, to be deeply sorry for ever having offended Me and desirous of being ever faithful to Me in the future.

Speak to Me now as you would to your dearest friend. Tell Me all that now fills your mind and heart. Are there any you wish to commend to Me? Tell Me their names, and tell Me what you would wish Me to do for them. Do not fear, ask for much; I love generous hearts, which, forgetting themselves, wish well to others.

Ask Me many graces for yourself. Are there not many you would wish to name, that would make you more happy, more useful and pleasing to others, and more worthy of My love? Tell Me the whole list of the favors you want of Me. Tell Me them with humility, knowing how poor you are without them, how unable to gain them by yourself; ask for them with much love, that they may make you more pleasing to Me.

With all simplicity, tell Me how self-seeking you are, how proud, vain, irritable, how cowardly in sacrifice, how lazy in work, uncertain in your good resolutions, and then ask Me to bless and crown your efforts. Fear not, blush not at the sight of so many failings; there are saints in heaven who had the faults you have; they came to Me lovingly, they prayed earestly to Me, and My grace has made them good and holy in My sight.

You should be Mine, body and soul; fear not, therefore, to ask of Me gifts of body and mind, health, judgement, memory, and success — ask for them for My sake; that God may be glorified in all things. I can grant everything, and never refuse to give what may make a soul dearer to Me and better able to fulfill the will of God.

Have you no plans for the future which occupy, perhaps distress, your mind? Tell Me your hopes, your fears. Is it about your future state? your position? some good you wish to bring to others? In what shall I help and bless your good will?

And what crosses have you? Have they been many and heavy ones? Has some one caused you pain? some one wounded your self-love? slighted you? injured you? Come aside and rest with Me awhile and tell Me how you suffered. Have you felt that some have been ungrateful to you, and unfeeling towards you? Tell Me all, and in the warmth of My heart you will find strength to forgive and even to forget that they have ever wished to pain you.

And what fears have you? My providence shall comfort you; My love sustain you. I am never away from you, never can abandon you. Are some growing cold in the interest and love they had for you? Pray to Me for them; I will restore them to you if it be better for you and your sanctification.

Have you not some happiness to make known to Me? What has happened, since you came to Me last, to console you, to gladden and give you joy. What was it? A mark of true friendship you received? A success unexpected and almost unhoped for? A fear suddenly taken away from you? And did you not remember the while, that in all it was my will, my love, that brought all that your heart has been so glad to have? It was My hand that guided and prepared all for you. Look to Me now, and say, "Dear Lord, I thank You."

You will soon leave Me now; what promises can you make Me? Let them be sincere ones, humble ones, full of love and desire to please

Me. Tell Me how carefully you will avoid every occasion of sin.

Promise Me to be kind to the poor; loving, for my sake, to friends; forgiving to your enemies; and charitable to all, not in word alone and actions, but in your very thoughts. When you have little love for your neighbor, whom you see, you are forgetting Me who am hidden from you.

Love all My saints; seek the help of your holy Guardian Angel. Love, above all, My own dear glorious Mother — she is your mother; O love her, speak to her often, and she will bring you to Me, and for her sake I will love and bless you more each day.

Return soon to Me again, but come with your heart empty of the world, for I have many more favors to give, more than you can know of. Bring your heart so that I may fill it with many gifts of my love.

My peace be with you.

Act of Faith

O my God, I firmly believe that you are one God in three divine persons, Father, Son and Holy Spirit; I believe that your divine Son became a man, and died for our sins, and that he will come to judge the living and the dead. I believe these and all the truths which the holy Catholic Church teaches, because you have revealed them, who can neither deceive nor be deceived.

Act of Hope

O my God, relying on your almighty power and infinite mercy and promises, I hope to obtain pardon of my sins, the help of your grace, and life everlasting, through the merits of Jesus Christ, my Lord and Redeemer.

Act of Love

O my God, I love you above all things, with my whole heart and soul, because you are all-good and worthy of all love. I love my neighbor as myself for the love of you. I forgive all who have injured me, and ask pardon of all whom I have injured.

Apostles' Creed

I believe in God, the Father almighty, creator of heaven and earth; and in Jesus Christ, his only Son, our Lord; who was conceived by the Holy Spirit, born of the Virgin Mary, suffered under Pontius Pilate, was crucified, died and was buried. He descended into hell; the third day he arose again from the dead; he ascended into heaven, sits at the right hand of God, the Father almighty; from thence he shall come to judge the living and the dead. I believe in the Holy Spirit, the holy Catholic Church, the communion of saints, the forgiveness of sins, the resurrection of the body, and life everlasting. Amen.

Act of Contrition

O my God, I am heartily sorry for having offended you, and I detest all my sins, because of your just punishments, but most of all because they offend you, my God, who are all-good and deserving of all my love. I firmly resolve, with the help of your grace, to sin no more and to avoid the near occasions of sin.

Veni, Sancte Spiritus

Come, Holy Spirit, send down those beams,
Which sweetly flow in silent streams
From your bright throne above.

O come, Father of the poor,
O come, source of all our store,
Come fill our hearts with love.

You of comforters the best,
You the soul's delightful guest,
The pilgrim's sweet relief.

Rest are you in our toil, most sweet
Refreshment in the noonday heat,
And solace in our grief.

O blessed light of life you are,
Fill with your light the inmost heart
Of those that hope in you.

Without your Godhead nothing can
Have any price or worth in man,
Nothing can harmless be.

Lord, wash our sinful stains away,
Water from heaven our barren clay,
Our wounds and bruises heal.

To your sweet yoke our still necks bow,
Warm with your love our hearts of snow,
Our wandering feet recall.

Grant to your faithful, dearest Lord,
Whose only hope is in your Word,
Your sevenfold gift of grace.

Grant us in life your grace, that we
In peace may die and ever be
In joy before your face. Amen. Alleluia.

Veni, Creator

Come, Holy Spirit, Creator come,
From thy bright heavenly throne!
Come, take possession of our souls,
And make them all thine own!

Thou who art called the Paraclete,
Best gift of God above,
The living spring, the living fire,
Sweet unction, and true love!

Thou who art sevenfold in thy grace,
Finger of God's right hand,
His promise, teaching little ones
To speak and understand!

O guide our minds with thy blest light,
With love our hearts inflame,
And with thy strength which ne'er decays
Confirm our mortal frame.

Far from us drive our hellish foe
True peace unto us bring,
And through all perils guide us safe
Beneath thy sacred wing.

Through thee may we the Father know,
Through thee the eternal Son
And thee the Spirit of them both
Thrice-blessed three in one.

All glory to the Father be,
And to the risen Son;
The same to thee, O Paraclete,
While endless ages run. Amen.

Spiritual Communion

I wish, my Lord, to receive you with the purity, humility and devotion with which your most holy Mother received you, with the spirit and fervor of the saints.

Personal Meditation

(*Before*) My Lord and my God, I firmly believe that you are here, that you see me, that you hear me. I adore you with profound reverence; I ask your pardon for my sins and the grace to make this time of prayer fruitful. My immaculate Mother, St. Joseph my father and lord, my guardian angel, intercede for me.

(*After*) I thank you, my God, for the good resolutions, affections and inspirations that you have
communicated to me in this meditation. I ask
your help to put them into effect. My immaculate Mother, St. Joseph my father and lord, my
guardian angel, intercede for me.

Way of the Cross

1. Jesus Christ is condemned to death.
2. Jesus receives the cross.
3. Jesus falls the first time.
4. Jesus is met by his blessed Mother.
5. The cross is laid on Simon of Cyrene.
6. Veronica wipes the face of Jesus.
7. Jesus falls the second time.
8. The women of Jerusalem mourn for our Lord.
9. Jesus falls a third time.
10. Jesus is stripped of his garments.
11. Jesus is nailed to the cross.
12. Jesus dies upon the cross.
13. Jesus is placed in the arms of his blessed Mother.
14. Jesus is place in the sepulcher.

The Memorare

Remember, O most gracious Virgin Mary, that never was it known that anyone who fled to your protection, implored your help or sought your intercession, was left unaided. Inspired by this confidence, I fly unto you, O Virgin of virgins, my Mother. To you I come, before you I stand, sinful and sorrowful. O Mother of the Word incarnate, despise not my petitions, but, in your mercy, hear and answer me. Amen.

Mysteries of the Rosary

JOYFUL:

1. The annunciation.

2. The visitation.

3. The nativity.

4. The presentation in the temple.

5. The finding of the child Jesus in the temple.

SORROWFUL:

1. The agony in the garden.

2. The scourging at the pillar.

3. The crowning with thorns.

4. The carrying of the cross.

5. The crucifixion and death of our Lord.

GLORIOUS:

1. The resurrection.

2. The ascension.

3. The descent of the Holy Spirit on the apostles.

4. The assumption.

5. The coronation of the blessed Virgin.

Litany of the Blessed Virgin

Lord, have mercy on us.

Christ, have mercy on us.

Lord, have mercy on us. Christ, hear us.

Christ, graciously hear us.

God the Father of heaven.   *Have mercy on us.*

God the Son, redeemer of the world.

God the Holy Spirit.

Holy Trinity, one God.

Holy Mary.   *Pray for us.*

Holy Mother of God.

Holy Virgin of virgins.

Mother of Christ.

Mother of the Church

Mother of divine grace.

Mother most pure.

Mother most chaste.

Mother inviolate.

Mother undefiled.

Mother most amiable.

Mother most admirable.

Mother of good counsel.

Mother of our Creator.

Mother of our Savior.

Virgin most prudent.

Virgin most venerable.

Virgin most renowned.

Virgin most powerful.

Virgin most merciful.

Virgin most faithful.

Mirror of justice.

Seat of wisdom.

Cause of our joy.

Spiritual vessel.

Vessel of honor.

Singular vessel of devotion.

Mystical rose.

Tower of David.

Tower of ivory.

House of gold.

Ark of the covenant.

Gate of heaven.

Morning star.

Health of the sick.

Refuge of sinners.

Comfort of the afflicted.

Help of Christians.

Queen of angels.

Queen of patriarchs.

Queen of prophets.

Queen of apostles.

Queen of martyrs.

Queen of confessors.

Queen of virgins.

Queen of all saints.

Queen conceived without original sin.

Queen assumed into heaven.

Queen of the most holy Rosary.

Queen of the family.

Queen of peace.

Lamb of God, who take away the sins of the world.

Spare us, O Lord.

Lamb of God, who take away the sins of the world.

Graciously hear us, O Lord.

Lamb of God, who take away the sins of the world.

Have mercy on us.

Let us pray. O God, whose only-begotten Son, by his life, death and resurrection, has purchased for us the rewards of eternal life; grant, we beseech you, that while meditating on these mysteries of the most holy Rosary of the blessed Virgin Mary, we may imitate what they contain, and obtain what they promise, through the same Christ our Lord. Amen.

To St. Joseph

Happy and blessed are you, O Joseph, to whom it was given not only to see and to hear the God whom many kings desired to see, and saw not; to hear, and heard him not; but to clothe him and to guard and defend him. Pray for us, O blessed Joseph. That we may be worthy of the promises of Christ.

Sorrows and Joys of St. Joseph

1. Joseph's hesitation in taking Mary into his home. The angel's revelation.

2. The Lord's birth in the midst of poverty. The angels singing glory to God in the highest.

3. The circumcision. The conferring of the name Jesus.

4. Simeon's prophecy about Jesus and Mary. He is to be the salvation and redemption of countless souls.

5. The flight into Egypt. Jesus is always at Joseph's side.

6. The return from Egypt and his fear of Archelaus. The appearance of the angel advising him to go to Nazareth.

7. The child is lost for three days. He is found among the doctors of the law.

To the Guardian Angel

Angel of God, my guardian dear,
To whom his love commits me here;
Ever this day be at my side,
To light and guard, to rule and guide. Amen.

Index

Personal Notes